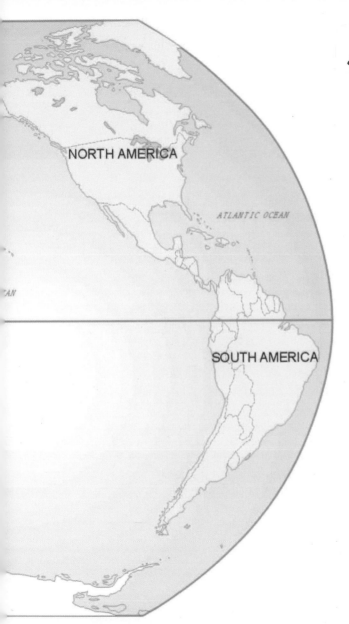

NORTH AMERICA

ATLANTIC OCEAN

SOUTH AMERICA

上海在世界的位置

Geographic location of Shanghai

Famous City in the East

SHANGHAI

东方名城

上海辞书出版社出版

PUBLISHED BY SHANGHAI LEXICOGRAPHIC PUBLISHING HOUSE

前几天，和几个国外来的朋友聚会在浦东金茂大厦，从数百米的高楼往下看，感觉是在天空俯瞰人间。外滩那些古老的建筑被灯光勾勒出曲折的轮廓，黄浦江在彩色的电光里流动，而远处的高楼大厦犹如一望无际的森林，磅礴的气势中带着一种神秘感。眼下的这个城市，确实浩瀚如汪洋，使我这个生于斯长于斯的上海人觉得既熟悉又陌生，既亲近又遥远。而国外的朋友则由衷发出感叹："这是世界上最美的城市。"

上海是中国人智慧和勤劳的结晶。千百年前，上海只是江滩上的一个小渔村，她衍变发展成一座城市，经历了传奇般的过程。十九世纪中期到二十世纪中叶，上海的变化和发展中凝着着中国人的辛酸和苦痛。这一段历史，可以说是中国近代史的缩影。积贫积弱的中国，从封闭到开放，是一个被动而屈辱的过程，上海的足迹印证了这样的过程。而二十世纪后半叶，上海走过的路也可以看作新中国迂回前进的历史。作为一个上海人，我对这个城市有着深厚的感情。半个世纪来，我目睹了她的意气风发，也亲历了她的徘徊和变迁。在已经翻过的历史册页中，她曾经步履蹒跚，也曾经踉跄无奈。然而在我的记忆中，上海一直是一个表情丰富的城市，曲折而独特的历史像一件七彩斑驳的风衣披在她身上，在中国，在世界，她的形象独一无二。而今天的上海，更是以日新月异的变化向世人展示她生机勃勃的形象。说上海是世界上最美的城市，也许有点夸张。不过如果说上海是最有活力的城市，我想会得到大多数人的认同。谁也无法否认，最近这十年来，上海正在发生巨变，变得越来越清新，越来越富有现代气息，上海的变化吸引了全世界的目光。

对于我们这个城市的特征及其变化，最为敏感的是摄影家。摄影家的镜头，能最真实形象地展示我们这座城市的现状。她的晨昏朝暮，她的喜怒哀乐，她的开阔和幽邃，她的博大和精微，她的古典和现代，她的变幻无穷的表情，她的生机勃勃的脚步，在摄影家的镜头中呼之欲出。照片是局部的，微观的，摄影家有时候能将一个局部的微观放大到纤毫毕现。相比文字，照片对现实的反映也许更为直观真实。无数个角度的捕捉，无数个瞬间的定格，把上海这座城市的表情凸现在人们的眼前。

上海是一个把梦想成为现实的城市。在摄影家的镜头中，我真切地看到了这种梦幻成真。上海的很多新景观，通过摄影家们匠心独具的拍摄，给人赏心悦目的同时，也让人感到惊喜。尤其是上海的夜景，由灯光勾勒出的城市轮廓能引发观者的无穷想像。上海也是一个可以使人怀旧的城市。曲折的历史在上海留下了无数独特的印记，譬如散布在上海各个角落的老房子，上海曾被人称为"万国建筑博览会"，这是殖民时代的印记，却也是人类智慧的结晶。怀旧不是为了否定新的生活，在新旧交织的景象中，可以感受到生活的进展。

一个城市的表情，可以通过人的神态表现出来。上海人的表情从来不是呆滞麻木的，即使是在最困苦的岁月，上海人的目光里也有对幸福生活的憧憬。现在的上海人，当然更是神采飞扬，男女老少，各有自己钟情的天地，他们毫无顾忌地把心情写在脸上，用简单的言语无法描绘这样的表情，而在摄影家的镜头中，上海人的表情被展现得淋漓尽致。

我喜欢上海，喜欢她的浪漫气息，更喜欢她的生机勃勃。但愿这本名为《上海》的画册能成为上海的一张形象的名片，让翻开这本画册的读者如临其境，被新上海生动的表情吸引。

于四步斋

A few days ago I was meeting with some overseas friends at the Jin Mao Tower in Pudong. Looking out from several hundred meters high, I felt I was surveying the human world from the sky. The old buildings along the Bund were outlined by lights and the Huangpu River flew in the reflections of shimmering lights. Further beyond stretched a boundless forest of high-rises. There is a kind of mystery in this awesome landscape. The city below looked like a vast ocean, making a Shanghainese like me feel both familiar and strange, intimate and yet remote. My overseas friends, however, just marveled at the view: "This is the most beautiful city on earth!"

Shanghai is the creation of clever hard-working Chinese. More than a thousand years ago Shanghai was but a small fishing village. Its miraculous transformation into a metropolis took place from the mid 19th century to the mid 20th century. But it was a bitter and painful process that personifies the modern history of China. Impoverished and powerless, China was forced to open its ports by the Western powers after its defeat in the Opium War. Shanghai embodied that chapter of history. The second half of the 20th century saw Shanghai develop in a zigzag course as did the rest of the country.

Being a Shanghainese, I'm attached to the city, having shared her joy, frustration and aspiration for over 50 years. To me, Shanghai is like a lady with rich expression, dressed in the vivid brocade of her own history. She is unique in the world. Today, she is wowing the world with her vigor and transfiguration. It might be exaggeration that Shanghai is the most beautiful city on earth, but it is widely accepted that she is the most dynamic city. Her transformation into a modern metropolis is attracting the world's attention.

Shanghai Impression

Zhao Lihong

People most sensitive to the changes of Shanghai are probably the photographers, whose lenses capture, in vivid detail, her varied expressions from dawn to dusk. Their pictures piece together a breathing image of this vibrant city, which seems to jump right out of the pages. Compared with words, photographs reveal the reality in a direct, faithful way and can capture the image of the city from different angles and in fleeting moments.

Shanghai is a city where you can make dreams come true. Through the lens of photographers, I can see how the dreams turn into reality. The creative approach of photographers also makes the city's new sites all the more fascinating. Shanghai looks splendid when illuminated at night, evoking viewers' imagination. It is also a city that brings nostalgia — her history etched in many old buildings that make the city known as the "Museum of World Architecture." These colonial-style buildings are nevertheless the product of human wisdom. Nostalgia is not a negation of new way of life, but rather, it makes the progress of time palpable.

The appearance of a city is often reflected in its individuals. You never find the deadpan expression of Shanghainese. Even in hardship their eyes shone with desire for good life. Today, you find contentment and happiness in their faces. Such an expression cannot be described in a few words, but a picture speaks a thousand words.

I like Shanghai; I like her romantic air, and I like her exuberant vitality even more. I wish this picture book can pass as the name card of Shanghai. Everyone who opens it will be absorbed and carried away.

目 录
Content

上海市容图
Map of Shanghai

上海市面积:6340.5平方公里
Area of Shanghai: 6340.5 square kilometers

上海市人口:1321.63万
Population of Shanghai: 13.21 million

曾几何时，"海天旭日"、"黄浦秋涛"、"吴淞烟雨"……原来是上海这个滨海小城的特有景致。然而，经过几百年的沧海桑田，更由于西风东渐以及革命成功，原来襟江带海的沪渎小镇已发展成为通衢纵横、高楼入云的东方大都会。昔日的江海胜景、沙洲烟霞已被交汇东西的现代人文景观所替代。特别是改革开放以来，上海城市建设日新月异，一座座标志性建筑拔地而起，荟萃成上海特有的都市风貌。

滔滔浦江母亲河，阅尽人间盛衰，外滩的万国建筑，既是旧中国人民屈辱的象征，又是西方文明登陆的标志。如今，站起来的浦江儿女描绘出更壮美的建设宏图，以人民广场为轴心的都市景观显示出上海建设者恢弘出色的大手笔。坐落在人民广场中心的上海博物馆，其形同宝鼎的建筑形式，象征中华文明博大精深，具九鼎之尊；而伴随她的上海大剧院，在华灯竞放的夜晚，如晶莹剔透的水晶宫，显示出浓烈的西方雅韵；地处上海西南角可容纳八万人的上海体育场堪称当今中国之最；亚洲第一高的浦东陆家嘴东方明珠电视塔是新上海的标志，她以大珠小珠落玉盘的奇巧构思，装点新上海，今朝更迷人！浦东国际机场是上海通向世界的又一门户，它如海鸥展翅，敞开胸怀，迎接四方宾客；刚刚落成的上海科技馆，其蜿蜒的身姿更犹如一条腾飞的巨龙，象征着"天行健，君子以自强不息"的东方精神！

今天的上海，以其五光十色、高楼栉比，日益显示国际大都市的风范。造绿护绿，保护环境，崇尚自然，也是现代上海景观的一个恒久主题。彩带飞舞的城市高架，上天入地的轨道交通是现代化都市的风景线，但上海建设者也没有忘记营造沁人心脾的绿，芳草萋萋的浦东世纪公园以及不断涌现的城市绿地，带给人们以春的退思；同时，上海人民追求现代，又不忘传统，从豫园九曲桥到南翔古猗园，从龙华古寺到松江唐经幢，保存完好的上海名胜古迹亦足以使人流连忘返，发思古之幽情……

绚丽多彩的上海景观无不透露出蓬勃的生机，人们常说，建筑艺术是凝固的交响乐，放眼春申大地，横跨浦江的南浦、杨浦大桥，其斜拉索桥身正像两架巨大的竖琴，在蓝天下弹奏出新上海建设的华彩乐章！

上海景

The Sights of Shanghai

In the days of yore, "sunrise on the sea," "autumn tides of Huangpu River" and "smoky rain in Wusong" were the wonders of Shanghai, then a fishing town by the sea. With the invasion of Western civilization and rapid urban development, Shanghai transformed from a small town into a metropolis with modern roads and skyscrapers. Its natural wonders were replaced by man—made wonders. Many of them were built in the past decade or so.

Huangpu, the mother river of Shanghai, is a witness to the city's transformation. The row of foreign buildings on its western bank once symbolized China's humiliation; today they are dwarfed by high—rises on the eastern bank in Pudong. Shanghai builders erected one monumental structure after another. The imposing Shanghai Museum in People's Square is shaped like an ancient bronze vessel; the nearby Shanghai Grand Theater turns into a luminous crystal palace after dark; the 80,000—seat Shanghai Stadium is the country's largest; while the Oriental Pearl Tower in Lujiazui, Pudong, is the highest structure in Asia; the Pudong International Airport, looking like a flying seagull, is the new gateway to Shanghai; and new Shanghai Science and Technology Museum resembles a giant dragon arising from the ground.

Shanghai is becoming an international city with modern high—rises, elevated highways and underground rails. Green areas are added each year to bring nature to the city. In their headlong race to modernization, local citizens haven't forgotten their cultural roots. From the zigzag bridge in Yuyuan Garden to Guqi Park in Nanxiang, from the Longhua Pagoda in Xujiahui to the Tang Dynasty scripture stele in Songjiang, heritage sites are well protected for future generations.

Shanghai's dynamic skyline bespeaks the city's brimming energy. If architecture is frozen music, as a saying goes, the two suspension bridges over the Huangpu River are like two upright harps playing a cadenza under the blue sky!

黄浦江两岸是上海标志性景观。高度468米的**东方明珠广播电视塔**和420米的**金茂大厦**是中国第一、世界第三的高塔和高楼。

The Huangpu River banks are dotted with such breathtaking landmarks as the Oriental Pearl TV Tower (468m) and the Jin Mao Tower (420m).

外滩位于黄浦江西岸,有"万国建筑博览"之美誉。
The Bund is known as the "Museum of World Architecture."

人民广场位于市中心,是融行政、文化、教育、交通、商业及休闲为一体的园林式广场。

People's Square — the heart of Shanghai — has the Municipal Building, Shanghai Museum, Shanghai Grand Theater and an underground mall.

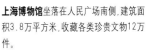

上海博物馆坐落在人民广场南侧,建筑面积3.8万平方米,收藏各类珍贵文物12万件。

Shanghai Museum has a collection of 120000 cultural relics and art antiques.

上海大剧院位于人民广场西北角,剧院设有大中小三个剧场,舞台面积达1600平方米,是目前世界上容纳面积最大的全自动机械舞台。

Shanghai Grand Theater has the world's largest automated stage and three separate theaters.

上海市人民政府大厦位于人民广场北侧,是上海行政中心。

The Shanghai Municipal Building is in the north of People's Square.

浦东科技馆在浦东世纪大道东侧,总建筑面积9.65万平方米,是一座以"自然、人、科技"为主题的大型综合科技馆,亚太经合组织(APEC)第九次领导人非正式会议在这里举行。

Shanghai Science & Technology Museum, by the Century Boulevard in Pudong and 96500 square meters in space, hosted the informal summit of the APEC leaders in 2001.

陆家嘴金融开发区与外滩隔江相望,是中国唯一以"金融贸易"命名的国家级开发区。
Lujiazui, an upstart business district in Pudong, faces the Bund across the Huangpu River.

南京路步行街被誉为"中华商业第一街",全长1033米,是外来旅游者观光购物的胜地。
The pedestrian section of Nanjing Road is a prime attraction to domestic and overseas travelers.

豫园商城位于上海老城厢，集古园林、城隍庙、商场于一域。商城汇集传统小商品上万种，有"小商品王国"之誉。

The Yuyuan Shopping Mall is a maze of traditional-style streets around the Yuyuan Garden and the Temple of Town Gods.

上海体育场位于市区西南的徐家汇地区，可容纳8万人，是目前中国规模最大、设施最先进的综合性体育馆。

Shanghai Stadium, which can seat 80000 spectators, is the largest and best equipped stadium in China.

上海图书馆建筑面积8万平方米，阅览座位3万个，藏书1320多万册，为世界十大图书馆之一。
Shanghai Library is one of the world's ten largest libraries with 30000 seats and 13.2 million books.

上海马戏城在闸北区大宁绿地旁，内部设施齐全，被誉为"中国马戏第一城"。
Shanghai Circus World in Zhabei District is claimed the best circus theater in China.

南浦大桥全长8346米,是上海市区第一座跨越黄浦江的双塔双索面斜拉桥,既是交通要道,又是观光景点。

The 8346-meter-long, cable-stayed suspension Bridge, Nanpu Bridge, is a city landmark.

苏州河全长125公里,曾是上海城市发展的水上通道。

Suzhou Creek, flowing 125km from Taihu Lake to Huangpu River, used to be the city's main waterway.

世纪公园面积140.3公顷,位于浦东新区,是上海新建成的最大绿地。

The 140.3-hectare Century Park in Pudong is the largest park in urban Shanghai.

延中绿地占地约23公顷,是市中心高架路下新辟的大型绿地,被称为"上海的绿肺"。

The green area along the elevated Yan'an Road Middle is dubbed the "lungs of Shanghai".

上海海洋水族馆位于东方明珠塔旁，总面积20538平方米，有万余条珍稀鱼类，其中的海底观景隧道总长155米，堪称世界之最。

Shanghai Aquarium, next to the Oriental Pearl TV Tower, has a 155-meter-long underwater tunnel for visitors to admire sea life.

虹桥经济技术开发区聚集了国内外众多的大型企业、公司和金融财团，是上海的对外贸易、外事活动和旅游居住中心之一。
Hongqiao Development Zone is home to many Chinese and foreign companies, luxury hotels and exhibition centers.

浦东国际机场占地32平方公里,距市中心30公里,机场设施先进,航站楼造型如海鸥展翅,夜景更为迷人。

The new Pudong International Airport, 30km from the city center, was built with advanced technology.

上海火车站位于市区北部的不夜城地区,候车大楼晶莹剔透,车站日均运客量多达8.2万人,是上海一大门户。

Shanghai Railway Station, which handles on average 82000 passengers a day, is the main gateway to the city.

东方绿舟——上海市青少年校外活动营地,位于青浦区,占地5600亩,融自然地形和人文景观于一体,集旅游观光休闲度假于一域的综合性园区。

Covering 373 hectares of land in Qingpu District, the Shanghai Student Activities Base combines education with recreation.

大观园在青浦区淀山湖畔,占地135亩,是根据《红楼梦》所描述的大观园景观而仿建,风光秀丽,是上海市郊的游览胜地之一。

上海植物园占地1200亩,引有2000多种植物,是中小学生的科普教育基地,海外人士最喜爱的郊游地。

Shanghai Botanical Garden features more than 2000 plant species, making it a haunt for students and expatriates.

上海动物园占地70万平方米,是市西郊一处良好的生态园。

Shanghai Zoo—a sprawling ecological park in the city's western suburbs.

Grand View Garden on the bank of Dianshan Lake is filled with Ming and -style buildings modeled on the classical novel "A Dream of Red Mansions."

以自然人文景观和现代游乐场为主的**佘山国家旅游度假区**。

The suburban Sheshan Hill is a national forest park and holiday resort with numerous heritage sites.

上海著名的旅游景点 —— 豫园 (始建于1559年), 位于上海老城区。
Built in 1559, Yuyuan Garden is the main attraction in Shanghai's old town area.

孙中山故居(1866—1925,中国革命的伟大先行者)。
The former residence of Sun Yat—sen (1866—1925), founder of the Republic of China.

清末曾为小刀会起义军指挥所的**豫园点春堂**。
The Spring Hall is where the Dagger Society plotted their 1853 uprising against the Qing Dynasty.

中国共产党第一次全国代表大会会址。
The birthplace of the Communist Party of China. It is here the CPC held its first congress meeting.

相传始建于242年的**龙华古寺**,是上海著名的佛教寺院。

Longhua Temple, which dates back to AD 242, is a famous Buddhist monastery.

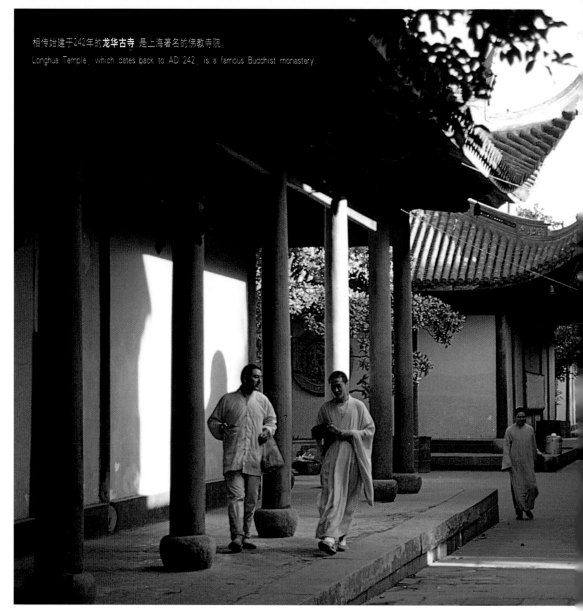

龙华古塔
The Longhua Pagoda

精美的玉佛寺**玉佛**。
The Jade Buddha Temple.

徐家汇天主教堂（建成于1910年）。
The Catholic Church in Xujiahui was built in 1910.

建筑雄伟、有"吴中第一"之誉的**嘉定孔庙**(建于1219年)。
The 783-year-old Confucian Temple in Jiading.

江南名园**古猗园**(始建于1746年),位于嘉定南翔镇。
The traditional Guqi Garden in Nanxiang Town dates back to 1746.

千年江南风，百里浦江情。

上海是个开放的城市，吴越文化根深叶茂，民族风情多姿多彩。跨入新世纪以来，经济文化日益发展，对外交流日趋频繁，五光十色的都市格调，使上海人民的生活翻开了新的一页。

有朋自远方来，不亦悦乎！作为一个中西交汇的文化名城，上海为世界各国的艺术使者来华施展身手提供了争奇斗艳的大舞台。中国上海国际艺术节、电影节、服装节……一个个国际性的文化佳节为东方都市吹来了西洋的风。中国的传统艺术也在中西文化的交流中大放异彩：昆曲好比旷谷中的幽兰，高雅脱俗；京剧则是国之瑰宝，魅力永存，她让西方人领略了东方文化的神韵和精髓。全民健身是市民生活的重要内容，无论是暮霭还是晨曦，随时可见人们体育锻炼的身影。热爱生命，崇尚科学，滚滚的长跑洪流展示的是前进中的上海人民昂扬的精神风貌。南京路有着"中华第一街"的美誉，有道是：十里长街，一路风情。其琳琅满目、别出心裁的橱窗布置，既反映商家招徕顾客的苦心，也体现他们高超的艺术创意。它与衣着靓丽的都市一族相映成辉，堪称上海特有的风景线。科技教育，上海历来领先全国，面向世界。作为新世纪的人才高地，上海吸引四方才俊，召唤各路英豪！

上海既有今日的辉煌，也有昔日的自豪。推翻满清，开创共和的孙中山先生曾在此地运筹帷幄，南湖红船的星星之火从上海石库门的小屋中点燃，多伦路文化街留下的是二十世纪三十年代上海文坛的风云际会，欧陆风情的衡山路休闲街则激发起人们对悠悠岁月的温馨回忆……

每当夜幕降临，流金溢采的上海，伴随着海上明月，犹如一颗东方明珠，日益焕发出新时代的迷人风采！

上海情

The Feelings of Shanghai

Shanghai is an open port where different cultures collide and merge. Yet, its indigenous culture, with roots going back to the ancient Wu—Yue period, continues to thrive. As the city progresses in the new century and expands its international exchanges, Shanghai people will embrace a new life.

Confucius said: "Isn't it a great joy to meet friends from afar?" Shanghai is a hospitable city and a famous cultural crossroad. It offers a grand stage for artists from around the world to show their talent. The China Shanghai International Festival of Arts, Shanghai International Film Festival, Shanghai International Fashion Festival, and Shanghai Tourism Festival have all become public holidays. During these exchanges, traditional Chinese art forms, such as Kunqu and Peking Opera, continue to dazzle foreign visitors like gems.

Physical exercise makes a large part of local people's life. Whether early in the morning or late in the afternoon, you see people walking, jogging, stretching and dancing. The huge crowds running marathon races illustrate local people's passion for health. Nanjing Road — China's best known shopping street — features stylish window displays, adding to the charm of the city. A pioneer in science, technology and education, Shanghai is a magnet to skilled professionals from around the world.

While savoring its success in urban construction, Shanghai spares no effort in preserving its past: the former residence of Sun Yat—sen, founder of the Republic of China; the house where the Chinese communists held their First National Congress; the homes of renowned Chinese writers on Duolun Road; and Hengshan Road, the street of leisure in the former French Concession.

As night falls, the city of Shanghai begins to throb with neon lights, like a sparkling pearl on the shore of the Pacific Ocean.

上海是历史上的江南重镇，是全国古桥最多的地区。位于青浦朱家角镇的**放生桥**，全长70.8米，为最大的古石拱桥。

hanghai tops the country in number of ancient bridges. The 70.8—meter—long Fangsheng Bridge in Zhujiajiao is the largest arched bridge from ancient times.

具有1140多年历史的**唐经幢**,位于松江区,是目前上海地面上最古老的文物。

The Tang Dynasty scripture stele has stood in Songjiang for over 1140 years, the oldest cultural relic of Shanghai.

上海有七棵**千年古树**,最古老的是这棵位于方泰镇有着1250多年树龄的银杏树。

There are seven thousand-year-old trees in Shanghai. This gingko tree in Fangtai Town was planted 1250 years ago.

南翔砖塔位于嘉定南翔镇,已逾千年而未拆修,保存完好,是国内罕见的古塔

This brick pagoda in Nanxiang has remained intact for over a thousand yea

石库门住宅与弄堂营造出几代风情,是上海人难忘的情结。

The so-called "Shikumen" alleyway houses evoke nostalgia about the city's past.

全国第二大剧种——**越剧**，为众多戏迷所钟爱。

Yueju, a local-style Chinese opera, still enjoys a big following.

舞蹈、杂技新秀不断,并屡获国际级奖项。
A number of Shanghai dancers and acrobats have won top awards in international competitions.

京剧、昆剧艺术,不断推陈出新,保持国萃魅力。
Peking opera and Kunju — twin gems of traditional Chinese art — remain popular in Shanghai.

广场文化成为群众所欣赏的街头文化活动。
Outdoor performances are a part of the city's mass culture.

丰富多彩的**上海文化佳节**

中国上海**国际艺术节**

Shanghai International
Festival of Arts,China

上海**旅游节**
Shanghai Tourism Festival

上海国际**服装文化节**

Shanghai International Fashion Festival

上海国际**花卉节**
Shanghai International
Flower Festival

上海国际**电影节**
Shanghai International
Film Festival

上海国际**茶文化节**
Shanghai International
Tea Culture Festival

上海的**体育运动**十分普及，体育成绩在全国名列前茅。

The city loves sports and leads the country in many athletic events.

上海的**服务行业**发达，人们生活非常方便。

Life is convenient in Shanghai, thanks to a we developed service industry.

上海吸引着世界各国，**中外交流**日趋频繁，外籍人员子女学校应运而生，目前上海有25所面向境外的国际学校。

As Shanghai becomes an international city, schools for foreign children have increased to 25.

2001年上海成功地举办了APEC会议。

The 2001 APEC meeting was held in Shanghai.

上海街头的**商业橱窗**汇成了一道亮丽的风景线。

Stylish shop windows add to the city's appearance.

上海目前拥有1896122个**商业网点**,组成了一个硕大的购物天堂。图为徐家汇商城。

Xujiahui — a shopping hub in southwestern Shanghai.
The city has over 1.89 million retail outlets.

上海已形成了一个专业齐全,能培养多层次人才的高等教育体系,这是又一批获得**博士**学位的毕业生。

Doctoral students celebrate their graduation. Shanghai has a well developed education system.

上海有"**世界建筑博览会**"之誉,风格迥异的各国不同时期的建筑,是上海城市发展的历史见证。
Many buildings from the city´s colonial past made Shanghai known as the "Museum of World Architecture."

创办于1917年的**大世界游乐中心**。

The Great World Entertainment
Center, built in 1917.

每天拥有百万游客的**淮海路商业街**。

The trendy, bustling shopping street of Huaihai Road.

绿荫覆盖下的**衡山路休闲街**。

The tree-lined Hengshan Road is a popular haunt for people after work.

融旅游、文化与购物于一体的**多伦路文化名人街**。

Once the home of many 1920s and '30s Chinese writers and educators, Duolun Road is now a sightseeing spot.

市郊农村保留着较多的传统生活。

Many families in the city's rural districts
cling to their traditional way of life.

位于东方明珠电视塔内的**上海城市历史发展陈列馆**,集历史、
文化、鉴赏、娱乐于一体,是旅游的新景点。
Shanghai History Museum, inside the Oriental Pearl TV Tower,
has a multimedia exhibition on the city's past.

迷人的**夜上海**

the night view of Shanghai

"我住长江头，君住长江尾"，水土地域的不同与经济文化的差异，往往形成一个民族不同的群体风貌。上海地处长江下游，有舟楫之便，商贾之利，由此招来五湖四海的宾客到上海谋生淘金。经过数百年的聚散离合，上海成了一个地道的移民城市——原籍本地人只占总人口的五分之一，其他则来自江苏、浙江、广东等地。在安土重迁的守旧传统社会，敢于背井离乡的各地移民，本身或多或少有其性格上破旧求进的特点，加上西方外来经济文化的影响，形成了上海人聪明灵活、不拘成法、重义趋利的性格特征。由于上海人较早接受西方文明的熏陶，存在经济文化方面的发展优势，因此具有一种地域的优越感，自我陶醉于都市文明中。但是，经过改革开放洗礼的上海人，如今有海纳百川的胸怀，就像当年上海本地人接纳八方宾客来沪安家落户一样，张开双臂欢迎来自五湖四海的兄弟姐妹！而现在上海的年轻一代也绝不是原来人们认为的宁愿挤在亭子间里相濡以沫，也不肯相忘于江湖、漂泊于他乡的小市民。好儿女志在四方，他们甚至乘槎浮海，飞出国门，到异域谋求更大的发展。

上海人寻求个人与社会、个人与集体利益与价值的最佳契合。市场经济的法则没有削弱传统的东方美德，幼吾幼，及人之幼；老吾老，及人之老，传统的伦理亲情在上海这个国际大都市里不断发扬光大。作为父母掌上明珠的少年儿童，他们享受着其前辈从未有过的优越生活条件，然而城市独生子女的特殊身份又为少年儿童的教育带来新的课题。桑榆晚景的老人如今有足够的闲暇，政府的夕阳工程，为他们的晚年带来生命的好时光；滚滚的自行车流是上班一族的集体写照，他们奔波于小家与单位之间，挑起事业与家庭的重担。上海人亦看重生活的文化品位，各种艺术均有忠实的知音，比如美轮美奂的越剧以其缠绵抒情的声腔，至今仍有众多的拥趸。沪上的芸芸众生相往往在街头得到充分的体现，衣着靓丽脱俗的少女，引领着时装的新潮，操着绵绵的吴侬软语，徜徉于十里长街，远胜于昔日的越女吴娃。上海人又最有投资理财意识，在证券交易所里，可谓"天下熙熙皆为利来，天下攘攘皆为利往"，但他们义利双修，当别人有难之时，上海人并不吝于爱心放送，从捐款到献骨髓，富裕起来的上海人对四方朋友依然充满古道热肠！

上海人

The People of Shanghai

Situated at the mouth of the Yangtze River, Shanghai has always been a shipping and trading hub, attracting merchants and craftsmen from all over. Year after year, these migrants struck roots here, eventually accounting for 80% of the local population. Most of them came from Jiangsu, Zhejiang and Guangdong provinces. Their pioneering spirit and ability to adapt to new surroundings, plus exposure to Western culture shaped their smart, pragmatic character. But their sense of well being also made them conceited and snobbish. With the opening and reform, Shanghai opened her arms to migrants once again, and her younger generations no longer cling to home. Many go abroad to pursue careers and dreams.

The people of Shanghai are seeking harmony between the individual and the society, between personal rights and public interests. The law of market economy has not impaired the traditional values and ethics. Children are living a kind of life their elders never dreamed of, although many families have to cope with problems unique to the one-child generation. Old folks are enjoying their retired life, made better by the government "Sunset Program." The torrents of cyclists during the rush hours reflect the daily life of local workers — the movers of our society.

Shanghai people demands high-quality cultural life. They are loyal fans to virtually all forms of art. The home-grown Yueju opera with its beautiful singing style enjoys a big following in the city. Impromptu fashion shows are staged daily in the street as young women dressed to kill strut the sidewalk. Shanghai people are keen stock buyers, spending long hours in trading halls to monitor market fluctuations. Their pursuit for money, however, does not prevent them from giving generously to the poor and needy. The newly affluent Shanghai people are as warm-hearted and hospitable as before.

人才交流市场盛况。

The seething crowds at a Shanghai job market.

上海60岁以上的**老年人**已占全市总人口的18％，健身是他们的主要活动。

成人仪式上的**中学生**（目前上海在校的中学生有79.54万人）。

People aged over 60 now make up 18% of the city's population. Physical exercise is their main occupation.

Students take an oath at a ceremony when they reach the adult age. There are about 795,400 high school students in Shanghai.

目前有**小学生**78.86万人。图为课外小乐队。

hildren orchestra practices after school. The

has more than 788600 primary school

ents.

从街头行人中可见**上海人**的时尚。

Shanghai is a fashion-conscious society.

The chore of life remains unchanged.

上海约有300万辆**自行车**,是许多市民上下班主要的交通工具。

Bikes are still a means of transportation for many local commuters.
There are about 3 million bikes in the city.

一户普通的双职工**家庭**。

A typical double-income Shanghai family.

把中医学推向世界的**医务工作者**。
Practitioners of traditional Chinese medicine.

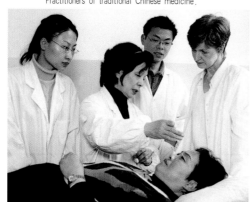

上海人的**境外游**越来越热。
Overseas travel is gaining popularity these days.

股市牵动着众多上海人的心。
Many Shanghai residents are stock buyers.

不同层次的**志愿者**纷呈都市，创导着上海人文明的风尚。

Shanghai boasts a large army of volunteers.

朝辉下的东方名城——**上海**。

Shanghai — a breathtaking and famous city in the east.

主编 EDITOR-IN-CHIEF

李伟国　Li Weiguo

副主编 DEPUTY EDITOR-IN-CHIEF

唐克敏　Tang Keming

责任编辑 CHIEF COPY EDITOR

谢新发　Xie Xinfa

摄影 PHOTOGRAPHERS

谢新发　纪海鹰　杨建正　达向群　潘文龙　Xie Xinfa　Ji Haiying　Yang Jianzheng　Da Xiangqun　Pan Wenlong

沈　良　何香生　郭天中　郭新洋　夏本建　Shen Liang　He Xiangsheng　Guo Tianzhong　Guo Xinyang　Xia Benjian

朱维祥　臧志成　邵雪林　张其正　杨绍明　Zhu Weixiang　Zang Zhicheng　Shao Xuelin　Zhang Qizheng　Yang Shaoming

祖忠人　郭一江　张　潮　黄柏松　赵中华　Zu Zhongren　Guo Yijiang　Zhang Chao　Huang Bosong　Zhao Zhonghua

策划 CHIEF DESIGNER

谢新发　Xie Xinfa

撰文 WRITERS

赵丽宏　祝振玉　Zhao Lihong Zhu Zhenyu

翻译 TRANSLATOR

王宁军　Wang Ningjun

封面书法 FRONTCOVER CALLIGRAPHY

邓　明　Deng Ming

美术编辑 ART EDITOR

汪　溪　Wang Xi

图书在版编目(CIP)数据

东方名城——上海/谢新发等编著.—上海: 上海辞书出版社, 2002.7

ISBN 7-5326-1010-1

Ⅰ.东... Ⅱ.谢... Ⅲ.上海市－概况－图集 Ⅳ.K925.1-64

中国版本图书馆CIP数据核字(2002)第045913号

东方名城-上海

上海辞书出版社出版　上海陕西北路457号　邮政编码:200040　上海辞书出版社发行所发行　上海中华印刷有限公司印刷

开本787X1092　1/24　印张3　2003年2月第1版第2次印刷　ISBN7-5326-1010-1/F·71　定价:30元

Published and distributed by the SHANGHAI LEXICOGRAPHIC PUBLISHING HOUSE, 457 Shanxi Road N, Shanghai 200040

Printd by SHANGHAI ZHONGHUA PRINTING CO.,LTD. ISBN7-5326-1010-1/F·71　Price:30yuan

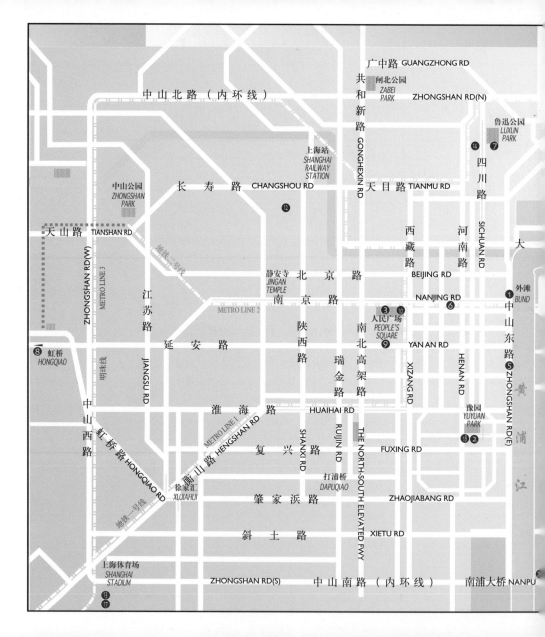